We See You

A MESSAGE FROM THE ANCESTORS

Don't Give Up

Chlarissa Harrison

Message from the Author

If you're reading this, you might be a young person facing some challenges right now—maybe even really tough ones. I had my own share of struggles growing up. There were days when I wondered why I was being punished, and times when I thought the world, or my mom, would be better off without me. For some reason, I could never picture myself as an adult. Even though I had such a strong mother, I still felt lost at times due to our circumstances.

I'm here as an example that things can improve. Hard times are just temporary blips in the grand scheme of things. Your attitude, focus, perspective, determination, and a bit of creativity can make a big difference in how your life can change. I am living proof of that, and I need you to be living proof too. I am still here for a reason. Part of that reason is to be here for you. You are here for a reason too. Your story, your dreams, your smile WILL make this world a better place.

You are loved. You are worthy. You are meant to be. You've got this. Don't let anyone dim your light.

With much love and light,
Chlarissa

Visit www.chlarissaharrison.com for additional resources.

In loving memory of Fannie, Jack, Ruby, Robert and Ronald.

HEY YOU. <u>YES YOU.</u>

We See You.

You are a light to this world and don't even know it.

HEY YOU. <u>YES YOU.</u>

We See You.

You have so much good
inside. You just need to
grow it.

HEY YOU. <u>YES YOU.</u>

We See You.

You think you are too young for your feelings to matter.

HEY YOU. <u>YES YOU.</u>

We See You.

Please hold on. One day
you will write your own
chapters.

HEY YOU. <u>YES YOU.</u>

We See You.

You've seen so much hurt
and pain that you don't
really understand.

HEY YOU. <u>YES YOU.</u>

We See You.

Is your mom on drugs or
does dad express his anger
with his hands?

HEY YOU. <u>YES YOU.</u>

We See You.

Are the kids at school mean to you, and you don't know why?

HEY YOU. <u>YES YOU.</u>

We See You.

Do you want to be left alone but your siblings want to fight?

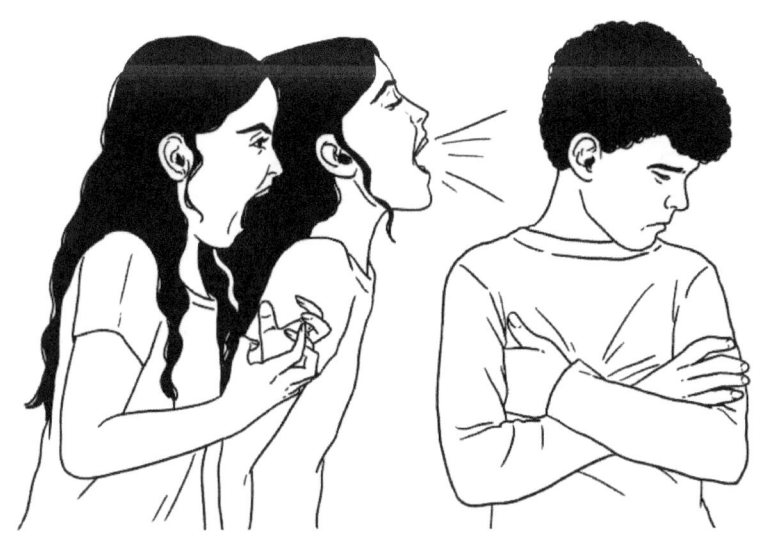

HEY YOU. <u>YES YOU.</u>

We See You.

Did it hurt when your favorite family member had to go to jail?

HEY YOU. <u>YES YOU.</u>

We See You.

Does your life at home sometimes feel like a life of pure hell?

HEY YOU. <u>YES YOU.</u>

We See You.

Were you taken away from your family and placed in a foster home?

HEY YOU. <u>YES YOU.</u>

We See You.

Do you want to run away
because surely it's better
on your own?

HEY YOU. <u>YES YOU.</u>

We See You.

Did someone close to you
die and leave this earth
too soon?

HEY YOU. <u>YES YOU.</u>

We See You.

Does the person who threatened you sneak into your room?

HEY YOU. <u>YES YOU.</u>

We See You.

Did someone bad touch you and you know it didn't feel right?

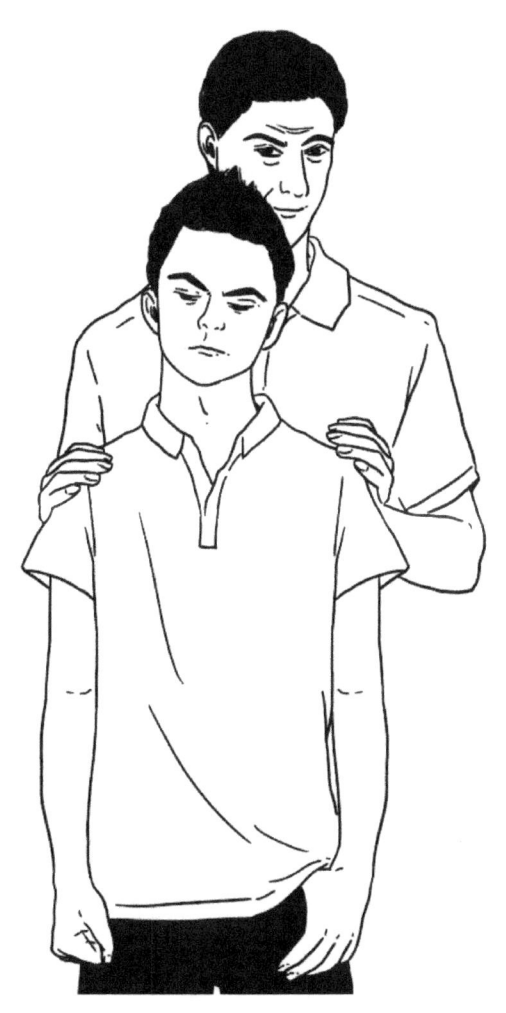

HEY YOU. <u>YES YOU.</u>

We See You.

Do you think differently from others or hear voices in the night?

HEY YOU. <u>YES YOU.</u>

We See You.

Does gang violence and gun shots make you fear for your life?

HEY YOU. <u>YES YOU.</u>

We See You.

Do you do whatever to fit in and find it hard just to survive?

HEY YOU. <u>YES YOU.</u>

We See You.

Do you want to be good but good is not considered cool?

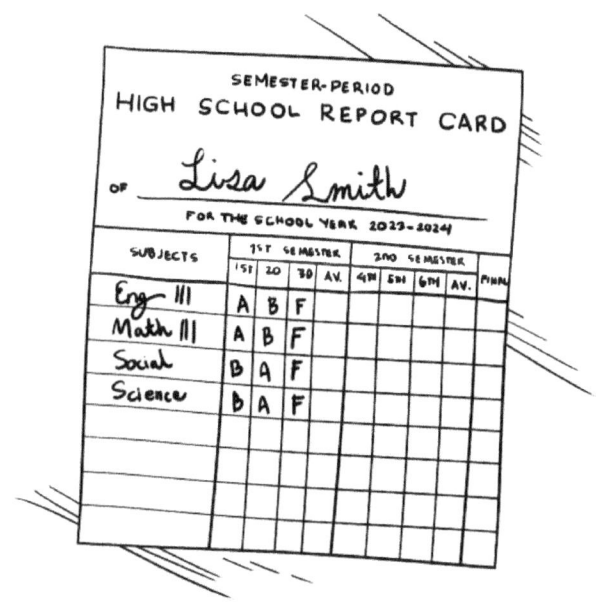

HEY YOU. <u>YES YOU.</u>

We See You.

Does your sexuality or looks make people treat you cruel?

HEY YOU. <u>YES YOU.</u>

We See You.

Are you always hungry because you don't have food to eat?

HEY YOU. <u>YES YOU.</u>

We See You.

Do you wear old clothes or have shoes with holes on your feet?

HEY YOU. <u>YES YOU.</u>

We See You.

Does the fakeness on social media have you second guessing?

HEY YOU. <u>YES YOU.</u>

We See You.

Do you feel like you want
to die at any given
second?

HEY YOU. <u>YES YOU.</u>
We See You.

We've traveled through
millennia with a message
just for you.

These words should be taken
to the heart because they
are true.

There are many things to say but one fact must be crystal clear.

Even when you feel alone, God and your ancestors are always near.

No matter what is going on around you, you are never by yourself.

No you can't talk to just anyone, but there is always someone to help.

If you don't have a trusted adult that you can talk to at home,

See if you can go to school and ask a counselor to use the phone.

There are many hotlines in this book that can provide hope.

Even if you don't want to leave your home, they can help you cope.

The worst thing that you can ever do is to keep it all inside.

Whatever it is you are going through is not worth suicide.

Suicide is a permanent end to a temporary, pesky problem.

How can you see the difference if you are not here to solve them?

Each day is a new day for you to try and try again.

If you don't try to heal, you'll never see yourself win.

God and your ancestors are truly depending on you.

If you take your life right now, you will never see it through.

Your ancestors suffered
through so much to get you
here today.

No generation has had it
easy, but they have always
made a way.

You are our greatest win.
You are our ancestral
redemption.

Because of you and your
light, pain will no longer
be our tradition.

You are the one that will
help us break these ugly,
stupid curses.

Your bloodline truly needs
you, so resist any and all
negative urges.

I know things seem hard
right now and like you will
never overcome.

Your heartbeat carries us
all inside with the power
of a million drums.

You have so much strength within. Please know how powerful you are.

You are descended from kings, queens, the sun, moon, and stars.

The light inside of your
heart and soul can rival
the brightest suns.

The blood that flows
through your veins can heal
millions to come.

Depressions, alcoholism, and other curses are going to end with you.

You are the key to unlock the chains. You are our dream come true.

Hold on, Chosen One. We see you and are forever with you.

Keep the faith. Keep the hope. I promise...

WE will see it through.

Crisis Hotlines For Youth
You are not alone. There are people who care.

If you are a child or teenager in crisis and need help immediately, please consult one of the following toll-free national hotlines or contact your local police or emergency services. All hotlines are free.

Boys Town National Hotline (1.800.448.3000)
http://www.boystown.org/national-hotline
Crisis and support line for children, youth and their parents, 24/7 and Spanish available. Multi-topic and issue assistance.

Childhelp (1.800.4ACHILD)
https://www.childhelp.org/
Provides 24/7 assistance in 170 languages to adults, children and youth with information and questions regarding child abuse. All calls are anonymous and confidential.

National Runaway Safeline (1.800.RUNAWAY)
http://www.1800runaway.org/
Crisis line for youth thinking about running away, for youth already on the run and for adults worried about a runaway. 24/7 help available.

Loveisrespect.org (1.800.331.9474)
http://www.loveisrespect.org/
Peer advocates available 24/7 to support teens with concerns about dating violence. Chat available thru their website, or text loveis to 22522.

Trevor Project Lifeline (1.866.488.7386)
http://www.thetrevorproject.org/lifelinechat
Provides 24/7 crisis intervention and suicide prevention services to lesbian, gay, bisexual, transgender, and questioning youth.

National Suicide Prevention Lifeline (1.800.273.TALK)
http://www.suicidepreventionlifeline.org/gethelp.aspx
Support and assistance 24/7 for anyone feeling depressed, overwhelmed or suicidal.

Source: https://www.stopitnow.org/ohc-content/crisis-hotlines-for-youth

Dedications

This book is dedicated to all the youth who lost their inner battle. You will never be forgotten. This book is also dedicated to the people who loved them and the people who continue the fight. Let's not give up on our youth and do our best to encourage them not to give up on themselves.

- In loving memory of my dear friend, Lexi Williams, of Gastonia, NC. Transitioned November 21, 2016 - At Age 16 ~ Jalen Harrison

- In loving memory of my dad, Dennis Cloninger, for his love and dedication to Loray Girl's Home. Thank you for showing us the love of God by your example. ~ Laura Taylor

www.ingramcontent.com/pod-product-compliance
Lightning Source LLC
Chambersburg PA
CBHW061715120626
46550CB00003B/1225